"What we do mean by the word "promimate" is, that because of convenience, of public policy, of a rough sense of justice, the law arbitrarily declines to trace a series of events beyond a certain point. This is not logic. It is practical politics."
—*Palsgraf v. Long Island R.R.*

"Hence, repetitions, free from all ambition."
—*Lyn Hejinian*

# Contents

# Post Hoc

When the bell rings twelve times
the grid begins; at the end of the grid
a punctuation and before long
action becomes possible

the word for action is delay
this way a point bleeds into the fabric
until it is revealed as a face
and the name of the face

will bring people to the fence
when a picture bleeds
he is not in time but time
is what you call it

then they will bring you money
and the bell has done its office
the body
permits you to leave the body

## Footnote

and if there is a grid
there must have been depth
if he becomes lost in a forest
there must be streets in the town

and objects in windows
that alert the shopper
to a power
he can never equal

hence to be flat
is to repeat flatness
against which the moat
the maiden and the apparition

stand in relief, the tale
can be used later
to illustrate the ill effects
of theft

# Sonnet

One who speaks of the multifariousness of voices
one through whom the voices speak speaks twice
once through rapt inflections breath on fire
once as metal fathers rising in the blood
the voice becoming wire and things said through it
thinner still so that
one who standing on the outside of a logos looking in
is one who sits within and reaching for the phone
arrives at speech his own by way of voices
he but replicates and theirs ventriloquized in him
are later written down: tundra, reindeer
permafrost that lives beneath the breath
all Spring partly vocable and partly simply cold;
the witness is unspeakable someone dead
who speaks the name a footstep leaves ahead.

# Subject Matter (a rewrite)

*for Hal Fischer*

I'm afloat on a sea, see,
and this sloop comes into view
that could be a seal
or a green furl of a wave

but it's not
it's a numeral
and there's this naked guy              and there's this naked person
who's not wearing any                   it illustrates

thing you could put your hand on
trying to illustrate a dream            whose name must be "Fig."
first you open the door                 a frame to modify a door
and it's the wrong room                 like a way of walking
                                        around a reservoir

you've been there before
then you climb a flight
and someone stares at you               filling in a form
this much is familiar                   with questions framed around it
                                        like where do you begin
stars form a story overhead             and instantly there are all these
cities made out of
minor metropoli                         stairs you could climb
and you are caught in it                or where to end, say
                                        in Tasmania at the horizon
trying to catch a bus                   in the furled leaves of a coleus
for which there is no change
chance never enters into it             a life force minus the life
some parts of speech                    equals number, one

and a fourth
I'm hardly necessary

to keep up appearances
but still I compose
red for the "ideal string"
black for the "concrete anchors"

gold
for where a ship falls
into a book whose name
is what the sea saw

it must have been me

two sentences dis-
cover a third city
in whose multiple talk
something like talk occurs

it is late spring
fog forms in the afternoon
I listen to you in Arcadia
where the light is gold

and in multiple otrings
you become a voice
it must be mine saying
ancient gong, ancient song

sing of land's end
when  you see two skies
one of eyes
the other of seas

# Song

Changes in the base
become changes in the violins
and violence the bass
portends a storm

that adumbrates a massing air
as fear
the crowd anticipates
and purchases

as though an ear
is program notes
an arrow in the fourteenth bar
delimits war

but what can rosewood know
that hand has not prepared
already in a knot left out
or hole left in

absent consonance
refusing stop or tempering
yet plays as if
an as if isn't

adequate, the market
sings all dissonance
as a single voice
the chorus echoes kyrie

at once a sign
and yet no figure
for what a crowd
thinks isn't music

but intention, gut
and aperture tuned
around an air, turned
into sound

sounds something
like an anthem something
like a word
or not

# Commentary

The one is neither top nor bottom
but in between partaking (though the one
presumes the other to be in darkness
of both) so that a grommet maker say

is holes he makes and what he needs
to justify making nothing to his son
who also comes to feel that work is just
something you do

the other is what you leave out
and ultimately have health insurance for
or not depending on how many stand to gain
by losing everything

but it returns a plural object
you can't afford and in the dark
declares itself like a simile someone uses
to get your vote, he too

is neither top nor bottom

# Mixed Aryan

The parochial blessings of an all too familiar ethnicity
Call to mind our youth in Winsor Parish
Which returns this windy night as a dream of parents
Who speak on the subject of our neighborhoods or the separation
Of prose and verse it hardly matters you are a white boy
In a green world power is held by the few we are enslaved
And so forth you pick up the theme from the genes
And submit it as your civics project in fifth period
For which you get a C from Mrs. Callous
But what did you expect
She's a teacher and probably a member of the Party
As they told you at the American Legion convention
Later you work for the Weenie King
And learn what goes on in Fairy Land
Radicalization comes slow among the painfully self-conscious
Where to see a tree is to become the wind
Or the music it calls to mind to see it with
It's hard to regard a tree as a commodity
But you learn and there are others handing you books
Covertly at first and then in broad daylight,
As your color changes the tax base remains the same
Soon you are almost Italian, then French, whole vistas
Of the underpriveleged are revealed in the pages of Max Weber
Which is very black and white
And soon these tropes have come full circle
To enclose you as the wind last night kept you awake
Only to heighten what the darkness gave you back, if fitfully,
And which continues in another form
Though you will seem to have invented it yourself
And this too is a blessing.

## The Form of Chiasmus; The Chiasmus of Forms

A number of positions to take with respect to the present. I am Providence. Some of the words you use to hang out the laundry are misspelled. Focused, sabbatical, acknowledgment, component and grateful are starched. Iris begins to emerge in tall grass; magnolias have been taking breath. Dogs graze, gutter water stands. It is the season of electricity.

The anxiety I'm thinking about. Do we have history or is this the obelisk? Is the use of this enough to join the Stamp Tax to Seward's Folly? Can I point and shout "avoid!" in an open field? They went west seeking not to be at home. They were the first to be belated. Others would follow in wagons.

I forget the simple things: the space occupied by chiasmus, the corner of whatever and whatever. Something that becomes you as you get older. His limp had developed in response to another limp. A causality of exigence blossoms forth into a self-evident slogan. They sell them because they exist. I pause at the top of the stairs and observe the red flag. He exists only through his envelopes, though he exits through a conundrum. Welcome to Darkness, you must be tired.

# The Second City

*for Cathy Simon*

Even though there are motorized conveyances
I am on foot, even though there is a map
I negotiate the streets by landmark

there are no landmarks
but a series of edges
common to several cities

the hill is in San Francisco,
the great shopping district
with its glittering windows

and esplanade before the fountain
is in New York
and the river with its bridges is in Paris

I'm working on the park
with its glass botanical gardens
marble pillars in the distance

leftover from the exposition
there is probably a hill
from which I descend

and arrive at the "market district" below
clearly indicated by the word "brick"
like those on the west aide of Buffalo

to make this descent
is to negotiate the terrifying grid
of hill cities, roads

dead-ending against canyons, barriers
where a street careens into space
and continues below

bearing the same name
so that a second city rises
out of the forgotten one

more pointed because not yet filled-in
by monument or palisade
the place where water touches land

and forms a line
the leaflike veins of streets
it is too late

for the bus
and I must walk from North Beach
to the Bronx or something with a 'B'

through the middle city
the place a middle occupies
when you are no longer familiar

and the buildings have only been seen
by night from a car
and by lights

I am afraid
someone will address me in French
and I will forget the word for myself

having so recently arrived
and yet to be a stranger
is to be swallowed up

without words
without glasses
and the envelope with a numbered series

in the second city
I live out the dream of the first
living neither for its access and glamor

nor dying from its disregard
simply talking towards the twin spires
of an ancient cathedral

like a person becoming like a person

# Thinking the Alps

It was by just such a state of logical perpendiculars
that "Bob" had arrived at this narrow pass
in the mountainous netherworld between being and time
and was preparing to reconnoiter the future
according to a long descending trope
of seven or eight partial figures complete with suffixes
until he arrived at the minimal camp below
its cookstove and portable toilet.

How had he come to this fork in what was up to now
a cliche ridden pursuit of normalcy with an unparalleled view
of deviance spreading out like conifers on either flank
their prepositions exfoliating according to a Persian design
the rug of which you see in Figure 3
where "Bob" decries a motif not unlike himself
as gatherer of leeches the better to invent
the trail which up to now he'd thought went straight ahead

but which appears to tarry, disappear and die
in sedgy grass among scattered tarns where to continue
is to be lost in an ancient folio illuminated by monks
parsing miracles in canons first intoned
on the one true cross, and "Bob" is but a ghostly sign
of a polluted cleft between Europe and Asia through which
Satan's armies drive a fetish plus handmaidens
into Paris just in time for mardis gras.

Suddenly vertical time bisects his gaze
suggesting action as a cure for vertiginous thought
and "Bob" moves forward pulling Melancholy his burro behind
hearing all the time the crowd's cascading cheers
from every canyon wall as he concludes the Bruckner fourth
mopping his brow and making his way over to the concertmaster
to shake a hand still vibrating from an undiminished chromaticism
in the works since Tartin's  Devil's Trill.

It's hard walking while conducting conversations
among ourselves thinks "Bob," yet where would we be
when faced with an actual business lunch composed of hands
holding knives and forks, their corporate bonhomie
reflected in certain iambics he imitates, voices
heard in falling water, crowds at airports, even these lines
must be saying something if we can stop them long enough
for a path to declare itself among infernal shades of type.

I'm not just anyone caught in a parable he boasts
for all the good it does him, product of the culture
that needs examples of aspiring men to build its cars from
still everyone needs a logo and I'm as good
as Andrew Carnegie on a stamp and better equipped
to be cancelled at postoffices by the sea
in which a postmaster has a taste for Cherubini
which he plays to salve the patience of the lines that form

reminding "Bob" of action whereupon he shifts his pack
and takes his first step since stanza four
destroying the Lake Poets in the process
while history breathes a sigh of relief and the owl
of Minerva takes flight, French horns in unison
strike up the autumnal largo from a woody glade
as workers go back to work, presses start up
and DeQuincy renews his quest for the snowy shack of Kant.

Crisp wind flutters through the latter half
of the Industrial Revolution as "Bob" is turned
into a lathe, screw, and spinning jenny making life tough
on the workers but easy on capital
which is why he sings without end, erasing intervals
in a landscape he just might buy some day, but for now
he is alone in a wood, in the story of the wood
and its conclusion that lies just ahead through those trees

which are made of wood, design of the sepulchre already etched
in a frieze by Brancusi which "Bob" hopes to inhabit
but which for now is memory thrown forward like the trail
he now concludes, drops his pack and stirs the coals
the better to become an ad for coffee,
I'm almost up to Modernism he thinks, and yet this solitude
prohibits me from being here, if only Melancholy faithful guide
could talk he'd make this ruined camp a home.

Holding steaming cup aloft he compares those cliffs
so recently declined to one of either sex
in whose airy gaze one sees oneself (are all these mirrors mine
"Bob" asks, or has the Forest Service placed them here
that visages might animate the trees they hang on)
as if we could be a prelude to ourselves
but that's crazy he thinks and besides I need to eat
and saying so pours water into sawdust for a stew.

Sun sets over campsight, pines shimmer in the astral twilight
that chills the weary traveller
with reminders of where he's not, and slipping into his cocoon
after humping up the coals "Bob" enters time
like a man stepping out of a long poem at the other end
and says goodnight to faithful Melancholy chewing grass
and proceeds into that land his author never planned to enter
source of all descents that once begun beget another.

## Lords Over Fact

I come to the letter eight
and start over
I come to the letter sixteen
it is the same thing

the same as one
done fifteen times
until the wings work by themselves
which is the letter two

and with this I take up the card
and write "two"
never again to begin
for the first time

and though I move steadily east
I continue the precession of four
doubled and redoubled
until I am almost not myself

so much a part of time
that number is only a tic
an old habit of one in its disguise
as three and its avatars

among leaves and the lame
and the trail so familiar
to the abject nineteen
unable to go on to twenty

he stands by the turnstile
at the sign of remainder
unlike zero the impossible one
partly the figure at the window

who has always gone and partly not
so that when you look out
it is six and seven, the letters
form a screen like prayer

that the ground might have something left
that water be allowed to stand
where it gathers in pools
nine

the sound of it roaring below the horizon
so that only dogs know
what is coming
they won't print this

because it is written by a dog
I speak for him
and translate eleven through fourteen
as quarters of the yard

ten is the forbidden zone
and even I draw a line around it
as it draws around me
something of its solitude

rain grows in the fold
between one layer
and the next
until stone is all they can say

so that to invoke the letter five
is to begin life again
feet form around it
and stars become points

that only eighteen can destroy
anything more than itself

is excessive and necessary
ten plus seven plus

the one we will have forgotten to pack
the minus that opens a rock
the rock that carries a key
telling of old weather

the time before weather
when the letters began to coalesce
and one thing entered another
often quite alone

# Rewrite

Once he had this face
and then he turned over
and had this other

"burned over 90 percent"
or simply getting older
of his body there were

faces yet to know
yet his own was not among them
he meant to say "one"

burning from within
a reaction to something he took
yet was actually getting older

and after all you burn
until there is no fuel left
you are left with a face

out of which you glare
others match theirs
to yours, it is

not enough yet once
in a dark mirror
you think at least mysterious

and walk back among them
waiting, and then the words begin
somewhat easier

Once he had this face
and then turned over
and was another

had been burned
over 90 percent of his body
or else his skin

fell in sheets from bones
that made a face
his own, he meant to say

I burn from within
I speak from a face
I no longer have

but after all the skin
is "really there"
you have this face

and people address themselves
to your glance, it is
not yours

but some words you think
to use against them
mostly friends

having skin also
where the mouth begins
the pain could not be described

# Statecraft

Conjure in the play the play sequence. He seeks some kind of remission the west beckons. So that once begun the way sustains a course, the ingenue is introduced. Second act a bone becomes a mirror of the hero, state arrives on horseback. Later lovers enjoy a tower before arriving at a fated bog; fireflies will light the forest way. Once inside already told so tell again these incidentals jewels the crown's a summary of. Sing this trail the many branching oak or by rivers have sung someone under stars and far from home one puts one together. Amazed as gaslight dims and curtain parts what is a child if not enamored of these folds the quest portends a sequel and begins to talk. Would stop if state could cease investing in farflung ports, imaginary islands these jungle props become a beer we like to drink back home. Lights in the trees our lay begets variations on a familiar tale: two brothers turned into their father's business one becomes the competition the other can't do without they fight. To keep the waking king asleep she spins out gaps in last night's plan she left to fill tonight.

Third act scene in gondola, girl recognizes leer as father's, dress as brother's, aunt as mirror's mirror, gondolier sings with intentions towards the Lido. Poet in Hell discerns life in stones so much confuses coin with what the coin is worth: a king's bald head bearing vines. Goes down long stairs others parsed before and from water conjures craft the state's long suppressed desire for ingenue. She's not to have an act without some maid attending to interpret her into troth and once violated prayer.

Hardly out of breath comes four the revelation scene mother's father's brother's uncle's ghost gives warning from the font our hero nearly dies of lassitude his double does the dangerous stuff. Cash invested in One Scene 2 accrues three times, three harpies on hand to palm their take. By five we're all worn out, tent folds leaving chorus aghast at bloody deeds till dawn. Night's piper tips the moonlit fence with silver all we came to see and hear is in this reed that silenced intimates anew. Innocence so made in author's image hasn't had a chance to speak at all and all night long reweaves bright tapestry one lying in a field espies the shifting field of heaven dreams inordinate and without guile. The folio concludes with pages torn enough to keep a scribe awake for years, but we know what frayed borders apostrophize: one to keep a poet locked in rhyme by law two to subsidize an army he may Pindarize three the love that drives iambics forward rocking horses four state sponsored muses nine in organdy and five the road that leads to Epos partly God and partly not. The rest becalmed read into lines all five can't anticipate is what an audience replicates their hypotactic way home conversations reinvent number not subordinate but undermine. This the folio foils and kings keep horses for.

# The Riddle

*"It's dark. But there's a moon."*

Desire is to hopeless the products you wonder
almost yet he wrote hidden and frankness as wit
yet
you find them everywhere "immaculate" for instance
the panel on the anal was infinitive
and
specifying a series of words beginning with "ill"
tokens future compensation, organs, hautbois, viola d'amore
but
wet left its card the boards remove Illinois
from ill-bred he was caused to become brutal
yet
a regular overlapping of petals or artichoke a playful
and rotund with mayonnaise or butter illumines
if
a logic can be adduced and elongated into witty stickers
a report imbricate used wrongly has not been writ
or
between volumes of air the report evaporates
they have supper the street remains a quiet mystery
then
tape measure and number two pencil exhaust
a paradox of number heaven-sent and given a bunker
nor
impossible as lifeguard reading Nietzsche
was rotund the flat had gained stature
but
and if then because weather fronts on logic
certain imperatives will lead to refusal
then
one will proceed however ill-mannered as a Volvo
or passion play little processional of children

for
without these assurances of metal how the struggle
can intersect in the sign and thereby busses coagulate
because
exactly in Idaho portion of the panhandle
down by sincere and chemicals vatic properties of liturgy
such
nations as this built half timbered and shot round
with smoking you found this based on volume plus
then
minus aura a stone that grows marks the landscape
not with Stanley but with Livingston.

# Commentary

In darkest sign two roads cross unexpected but nevertheless is never plus less

In dark sign son and father coincide as less plus the

In dim light desire in sight also contains father, son, state is often more

In designing sign father for son, sign son for mother, sign hidden the more adduced in less

In witness where two roads cross empire hidden sight and in sight signs blindness there's only one of us

You here in darkest witness impressed in products unexpected but here you become less and less

Infant is to hopeless as helpless is to power X marks where son is to infant but more

Immaculate we say white at a corner or angle of empire what is hidden is also below

But in desire he writes X marks where he is yet between volumes then to become unseen as he is unsighted

If in either desire or satisfaction one event tilts to the next then we are immaculate we are more

In this we have maps plus X plus instruments they have lifeguard, Volvo, metal, and Stanley

In unsightly darkness crossing products with desire soon it will not be Africa only sign

In terms of sign more is hidden where less is product S marks the spot

In plus if to encounter number at two roads more continues though it's hidden

In desire is hopeless wonder yet sign goes on as S as X and as plus but one is also one

# Cloud

It doesn't show
but I'm making up a new word
to replace Plato
with a tape delay

but that's two words
one for you and one
the first makes possible
impossible to say

in unison but in time
a cloud will return
in the same shape
and you call upon

an Ion to verify
an elephant but he'll say
anything
the power of suggestion

is water
he never forgets

# Elsewhere

Over here in window
I prepare resolution once again
thin streams of water coat the glass
that visibility sets out to destroy

by turning on a light, slowly
I become solid
and without friends
in whose voices dispersal

is what they call me
not without affection
still
the names of those trees

slide away
so that almost a cube
I will a body into words
and talk like one

using rain as guide
all night it dropped on the roof
I left myself
to imagine

and then while the world
was still tipped on its end
he slid back into sleep
and the inner ear

was left to explain
how it was done, it was
not for me to know
as these shapes

(lozenge of yellow and white plane
green triangle
discerned through frosted glass)
are almost always moving

threading
the rectangle of vision
with a fable made mostly
of weather

one
you will one lose yourself
two
become the opposite

three
carry the message
known as elsewhere
into the library.

if I knew which volume rhythm appears in
rhythm would appear in
a square of light

# Commentary

On some days you can see the edges
you seem to have solved that problem with the cord
and look how the bottles fit on the shelf
even the voices calling in the street

are intended for you
and you listen for advice
because let's face it
the leaves are signs

the lamp signifies a change
not an object in itself
although it sat for years
on the edge of the dresser

and cast a multicolored light
onto a white doily
the trees, on the other hand,
have no such permanence

they replace air every second
as they consume shape
size and quantity
to say that they "need" water

is to step out of yourself
as a man having a dream
is inclined to fly
clearly impossible

let's have the next slide
the ear actually occurred
hearing the rain on the roof
in the middle of night

he felt the room spin in circles
so that closing his eyes
saw a sea by day unstable
by night, waking

was a table of black
the way a cube
defines a jellyfish existence
this day

I learned the principle of windows
which tomorrow will seem again a wall
but between them this line
draws the arrow to N

and weights a fable
with the plumb of something seen
the yellow umbrella in the corner
is one such example

# Words Without History

I'm on the far shore looking back
what preceded is none of my concern
what lies ahead is someone else's idea

and despite the sign
What You Carry Can Be Replaced
Others Have Died In Its Creation

I don't mind carrying the load
the landscape is bound to be flat
never having been allowed to grow

never having wanted
not to be itself
and lacking connectives between be

and itself makes each journey shorter
than the last, no doubt to others
I appear flat as well

visible from the front
where they hang my name
but from the side

I am an "I" etched against black
almost invisible except for the quotes
that form a halo around

the place I must be, what I say
is no longer my own
but something that grew

from the voices of others
and came to resemble them
in my face

so that I carry them with me
in a flat world without smoke or cloud
or a thin rippling stream

that saying nothing
witholding nothing
goes on ahead

and I follow

# The Last Word on the Sign

*"contingency is correlative to a necessity"*
*—Husserl*


Some things have to be sitting on four legs
to bear the weight
of one
who could sit anywhere but prefers

where he is
was never forced
happened to come along this way
followed a pointing finger

and sat
one part plasma
one part what he sat
to think about

what he thought
was in
was red
and how it blushed

becoming something more
than "out"
the blue without which
water is a table

between them
difference forms on a slide
like a chair made out of flesh
in the phrase "I'll think on it"

which not to sit perfects
though I was here first
and have my receipts
I needed just this much

to explain it to you

# The Penultimate Word

He enters the world wordless
discerns a tree through the eyes
of the word tree
and they give him a chair

made partly of wood, partly of air
the first is a shell
for the S that points at itself
and sounds like there

the next is not outside, not
core nor cloud but not one
or more
the chair has not to be himself

to sit in
in which the idea of a worldless I
takes up the winter and by the spring
is a convention of weather

the word the weather needed
just to be himself
and the protective outer clothing
necessary

satisfaction marks the agreement
between rain and water
which falls today
in both forms equally

equally filling
the empty dog dish
this is the sign
of something extra

to which I am attached

# The Antepenult

The caption under
the photograph on the first page
of the second section
of *The New York Times*

announcing the cast
of the recent production
of *Le Nozze di Figaro*
at the Glyndebourne Festival in Britain

did not correspond
to the photograph of Mick
Jagger and the Rolling Stones
at a Press Conference

held at Grand Central Station
announcing their forthcoming tour
"Steel Wheels" for 70 million dollars
put there by mistake

but it was close

# Troth

It's not much of a choice
cut off his head with a really big sword
return next year
and he cuts off yours

forests intervene
trails lead into other trails
green stands for everything
the trail isn't

home with its turrets of gold
flags bent in the wind
recedes behind a stencil of hills
why

repeat the instructions
to the letter
to the letter
is it

a. for what the old woodman wants
b. before c
in a sequence demanding
a cup

and what's inscribed
around its rim
he's been especting you
and you

know his bony finger
pointing towards a spire
is all there is
of this forest

but signs are intentions
and you follow
besides she's bound
to be attractive

and it's a year later
this is the test:
to be true
not to the tale

as it becomes you
but to the choice
of losing your head
for its telling, troth

takes you to Trotsky
in a book without ideas
they deal with him from a distance
so it is written

# Century of Hands

The libido portion goes haywire
I fly off in several directions
and occur to myself
at the same time

in a number of colors
alors, I am a liquid substance
and receive letters from the sun
tiens, I believe a rock

is an intelligent machine
with designs on my inside
first the spleen
like a red tongue, then the liver

known as the bad aubergine
no one must know this
I whisper in a bent-over posture
to my mirror

and when they turn off the water
and lock all the doors
it is my books they refuse me
my map my gun

who is it has made my tongue so treacherous
that the most seductive caller
is told I am an aging widower
who has moved out of town

who plants these deceptive fungi
next to the fence
that I may be tested again and again
in the crucible of taxonomies

may he be prevented from witnessing
my Nova, light pouring
out of the sky, may he
become doxa, the speech

of clerks and shopkeepers
that we become the words
for lathe and forge
pounded out of capital

I exit history through the rear
the only orifice left unguarded
what was intended for me
is a bomb in a bouquet

and I am its sender, either way
I return
as the one who opens the box
and checks the numbers

filthy messenger
of that effulgence destined only for me
I make the words
dance, I make the silence

# The Terror

When we come full circle
to the rose garden in the Imaginary
will we remember the Terror

the names whose crimes are invented
in order to have something else to kill
the King's absent face at the window

across from the dock
the names of the trains
that run on time for the first time

I think of this
when I read of the stupidity of princes
with breakfast, by midday

the stock market has made one of them rich
and part of my breakfast
has bought his lunch

and paid someone to espallier
his roses across an adobe wall
they never die, the pronouns

become so malleable
they refer to anyone
but never oneself

something must be exchanged
for the privelege of joining a word
to its source, something must not fit

for its replacement to be the wrong size
then the Terror begins
in the hot weather

when they drain all the pools
and the bidding wars keep them empty
the contractor who will inherit the earth

is figuring out out how to do it
even as we speak
just listen

# Turkey Dust

## 1

There was the present. I acted on it, and it made me new. Wind came down, also leaves. Motion interprets the one walking towards it. The parrot could be heard addressing the passersby from the telephone pole. First there had been the experience of looking at the clock. Ten-ten indicates the time represented as time. Seven o'clock indicates the news. All along the street vendors hawked their wares while a toothless man opened his palms to the reader. Without causality a number is only so manystones, so many teeth. A city forms around towers of belief. Their point is that the sky is not enough. Radiant signage announced our passage into the desert.

## 2

The sister testified that she lived there continuously from August 1 to August 1; that the man who had lived there and ran the store prior to August 1 had made no complaint to them about the dust; that around July she noticed something "unusual" in that "there was turkey dust"; that she noticed this dust when she went outside at 6:30 in the mornings; that the dust was thick "lots of times"; that it would depend largely on the breeze; that the dust would be heavy three or four times a week; that it would last an hour or an hour and a half in the morning; that she could see dust on the outside; that in the the evenings she would not know the dust was rising "unless I was out"; that "if I was outside I could see the dust was rising and coming our way"; and that at times she could smell it inside the house.

3

In this farflung riven backwater a green bird torques haplessly passersby to look and exclaim ciao. The fragrant denial of voice and body so merciless to exclude portions of his readers exclaim Anglo-Saxon and postage stamps there on the field at Dunsinane. Your readers must perambulate. Has a warp like flue through which gasses also charts and wax paper foetid like undiscovered garments and mouldering under centuries. Their bodies also reeking wisdom a riddle also a question. The quality indeterminate (forced landing) smells percolating from bed wall spoons out of drawers pills from a bottle in the waystation of (perish) fabulous and small monsters who ascend in an elevator the pinnacles of found hospitality.

4

In these critical waters the space between one and won is a hairline fracture. First there was difference then there was not difference then difference returned in an opposable thumb. These events happened in a space of oh say twenty years. The question is not what separates any two shards but the meaning of the space between them. Meaning of the vessels, meaning of the throwing of the vessels, meaning of the excavation of the site, funding of the meaning of the excavation etc. He had those "little brown ones" to distinguish the "little white ones," and the crowd roared its approval whatever it meant. To collect the remnants was not an idle task although he heard the pun and laughed to himself. The "fragrant denial of voice and body" was apparent in the way he carried himself. Little stories upon which the law bears the edifice of state that when examined explodes into a fine mist. This is what an explosion never feels like.

# Song

The bowl frames the wind song
the tree branch brackets
Mt. Tam wind comes
from the west, rustles

chimes hanging
from a limb the cat climbs
as rain begins, the line
tries to gain

on sequence, fails
to frame the window, song
make music out of wind
sing to her this motion

neither tending towards
nor caused yet love links
bowl (a gift) with wind
it stands against

# Hypothesis

I began
scattered
recollected in parts of the city
the parts that remain useful

rusted shed
mossy creek bottom
deserted produce district
narrative begins

in friable youth
loses itself
in uncomfortable consonants
gh and cc, water

is an ancient hypothesis
earth floats upon it
"like a piece of wood
or other flotsam"

in my second book
the censor permits us
to see everything
I refuse rehabilitation

and leave with parents
for the beach, sand looms
large in a life made up
of the opinions of others

for with dispersion
we become compound
and take on the protective coloring
the desert demands

blue heron which is grey
great egret against green pine
grebe that ducks for crustacean
in dispersion water sounds

like everything else
a crowd of mocking boys
in the balcony and the film
about an ape and a helpless girl

injustice begins
in the way they tell the story
of my story
I am a monkey that coincides

with a small organ, in the telling
I happens
discovered among cattails
forbidden words

or the olfactory richness
of basements, something indistinguishable
from something else
is handed around under the table

# Utter Mimesis

And we look out on Lake Premise
from the deck of our A-frame
high in this forest
of the alpine sublime

neither one nor another
nor the sum of our parts
falling into the sun
as into the green sun spreads

across flat water
mist rising as a faint trumpet
announces Stage One
one seeks

a telltale wake
to alert a boy
to a watery script meant only for him
that he might leave reading

and become the book
become the author the story
describes the trials of
among unfamilar pines

Stage Two begins
when a Zero
intercepts a Messerschmitt
on the ceiling

and the war comes home
Spitfire at twelve o'clock
Focke Wulf behind alarm clock
this is Audie Murphy actor

and author speaking
the lines he knows best
in a war written in water
which two boats make parallel

each boy has a dinghy
docked by the unprintable wharf
he dangles his toes
and something nibbles

thinking it is bait
these have been
sentences produced
by the editors of the Hard Boys

that white kids
become a son
or a pair of detectives named Arthur
the author is not his real name

but I am
see here
M is Men
and W is upside down

water becomes more than a mirror
when the wind rises

# Answers from the Penetralia of Archeology
## A Translation for Norma Cole

Before A came a wraith like A
remembering you
twice eyes, twice arms, legs
and the absent body
that a body bears to be
more than it is

being dead
they are naturally restless
finding themselves in agreement

when the voice is in pain
the body has already given itself
to air
and refuses to speak of anything
different as different

the same man has written to another
that he might not say
what would be misconstrued
were it overheard
framing the words
as if without a listener

in a hollow log
one places a letter

the A within the A
mumbles instructions
for the next pyramid to be built
what is left over
falls in upon himself

over the water
across wastes

nothing in the desert
is left over
even the sand
is an example

the smoke from a fissure
in a rock by a spring
where no one has been
could be a voice a line
in a vase
has been read both ways

all of the pilgrims
carry a book in their heads
or each of the pilgrims
carries a book of the head

as a sign

there must have been birds
forming an A, one
glides on the next
and when they speak
it is said
to be the language of birds

a seam in air

the lyric was impossible to read
it was like applying language
to my skin
everywhere where there was no sound
was a wound

choirs
where the birds once were

sighted
from the thing seen

# Proximate Cause

In the case of margins
I fill the vase with iris
in the case of Arabs
a plank fell into the hold

these cannot be proved
yet at the end of a lake
will be all the lake has undergone

a boy has been placed there
to be its result
to be a line of silt

it is written:

former president writes memoir
revealing whiteness
diplomat publishes memo after thirty years
revealing whiteness

that the ship was lost in fire
and its evidence consumed
that the spark could not be anticipated
shines on an otherwise blue

horizon fills the horizon

though I can't prove this raised voice
in anger is my own
in a dream I am rowing a voice

through an audience in Morocco
a burning board falling into a dark square
will ignite a ship

if it can be proved
that an act of God, the King's enemies
or the restraint of princes, people

in collision, an act, neglect or default
are not the result
of a single voice raised

if it seems to be a bundle of newspapers
but turns out to be dynamite
or a man sleeping in a blue blanket

and a car runs over it
then the explosion may cause a scales
to fall on an innocent janitor

harming no one

three ripples equal three boys
one of whom lives to tell of it
nor do I comment on the word "unreasonable"

it is reasonable to assume fire in a pan
results from combustables
piled in a corner or a proximate flame

from a sleeping person
who goes out on a negligant journey
in order to sleep

but what is written in sleep
still burns
I have marks

# Propter Hoc

The sign of the center
mandates a center
jungles fall around it
and in the last days

we are sure to be first
I that am a center
sustain my post at the outpost
the male of the species

will act accordingly
marking its trees, an open field
beyond the smokestacks
is the sum of its perceivers

yet a man found at the site
will be assumed to have thrown a stone
and a person found in a book
will be forever named as the person in the book

one could not have spoken it
but could make it resound
as though a rock
were known by its circles

or an island by its print in the sand
we needed the map at first
until we memorized the lines
the last island became a peninsula

and the river gave way
to the ocean at last
then we memorized the trees, apparently
our cries could be heard from here

as birds
the We who orders these things
will never be misunderstood again
and writes it down

but a baby born in the Dragon year
is the commune
and will misunderstand everything
surpassing legend

if she appears in flames by night
we are the fuel
if she appears all clothed in white
we are the coal

this too falls
under the sign of the center
but she makes a sound
we don't recognize

upon which nothing serving the city
can be built
and this becomes the city
after the fact

# Analogy of the Ion

*for David Bromige*

*"If the world, instead of being beauty, were nothing but equally large unvariegated boulders, there would still be no repetition."*
—*Kierkegaard*

## I

There would be a first word and it would permit the first one to speak it.

It's hard not liking a philosophy made out of chairs and slabs the force of an idea becoming gradually a sentence and later you meet for lunch.

They arrive at the Brick Hut as an afterthought the airport was closed because of a quake he barely got off the ground is it the food or the name he prefers?

Following writing a faint ghost in green of what he said for a brief moment fills the screen and then dies.

Up there in Sonoma, down in L.A., back in the Midwest, out in Wyoming she studies the law where jurisdiction does not occur in the same place twice.

What will he say according to the rules you show interest in the other person's not having paid any particular attention and with such enthusiasm.

The circle is the house is the measure is the map is the sky.

Paper wraps stone, stone flattens scissors, scissors cut paper you could also write them and achieve the same effect.

He achieved a materiality that only metaphysics could explain.

They became friends of mimesis, each referring to himself by the other's name.

He wrote out of a desire to stand over history, one foot in the Adriatic and the other in the Lago di Garda, while soldiers made their way up treacherous mountains of typographical errors and

and false etymologies.

Other news included how to wave at the judges.

To distinguish between the penis and the phallus he wrote his father's name in his notebook and then tore out the page.

By gradually gathering parts of various board games from thrift shops he created new objects out of vestigial commands no longer linked to the tiny swans and barns and cups that had been their actors.

In the north in the south in the west in the east there was still the position of in.

The opinion spoke of the failure of the arrangement to achieve intrinsic and continuing reality,

But we exist in the belief that toothpaste and mayonnaise shall never occur in the same sentence.

It was a familiar story the lover seeks to be comforted nothing will suffice maybe by singing someone will hear him the autumn winds blow the leaves over his guitar etc.

The earthquake had served warning that next time it would take out Glendale and half of the Burbank airport.

They had contrived a solution to the problem of the homeless by reinterpreting their plight as a need to assert their freedom to chose not to come indoors.

He hankered after a good hamburger.

You can erase these mistakes with ease became you can erase these mistakes with ease.

Each morning the city unrolled its plan slowly from the hills down to the bay as the fog lifted and the neighbors opened their windows.

Epos is not cold history he wrote slash he writes.

And behold our dynasty came in between an oil shortage and an oil glut this will be recorded somewhere.

Had he been wasting his time making empty statements of fact was the only way he could frame his discomfiture over the absence of interrogatives.

The grid falls apart where S meets A, but it is also the oldest intersection in town.

# II

The brochure defines the project but what does a project define?

The sound of its (a city of indeterminite size, aspirations or tax base) conveyances drowns out the harpsichord.

After which he could reflect on a certain dynastic calm that came with his pension.

One of the projects involved cutting down a tree to make way for a magnetic recording center, the tree plated with steel and re-planted with a tiny speaker that plays country western songs.

After all it was a replaceable culture and so long as you avoided reference to the structure anything could be said for the first time.

You think of all of the relevant cases In which thinking is possible (on the spot, in reflection, out loud) and imagine the same object.

He puts a bag over his head and counts to an unimaginable number.

He first conceived the world as a shape discovered in the Oz books and later as a geometrical theorem it was empty and could contain anything.

You could imagine a world that begins once they cross the Red Sea or else one that mimics the diaspora itself, but scientists now believed that the waters parted by natural causes so another world was born that incorporated the previous two.

Another project involved a series of Stonehenge-like pilings that had become a popular place for the Chancellor to have his picnics.

His marginal comments were gender-neutral, but she wondered when a pen was not a pen.

Defectors were signalling their decisions in carefully worded statements leaked to the press the implication was that power had been handled badly they included pictures.

He liked the idea of photographs better than the actual products and justified his distaste by reading some of the recent literature.

What he meant by A at that early date was not what he meant now he was at pains to point out in a series of published disclaimers.

So far their new vantage had been framed by the great oak worm disaster that even if it didn't kill the trees left a great deal of their structure exposed for future generations.

He had been mentioned in an oblique context and because it was phrased badly felt obliged to dissociate himself if not from the sentiment at least from its grammar.

Up here, up there, up ahead, up north, there remains the position of down.

A code violation was being repaired by a man in the back of the house listening to the hearings while in the front another listened to the Beatles she couldn't compute.

A critic so famous that his review had forced Satie to confront him physically on the Pont Neuf.

Only the measure of squirrels running across the roof controls the deployment of his phrases.

A history is also a story the word is unambiguous on this point.

# III

If plus heat
three as three
a man marked man
is inconclusive
and woman swims
simply open
then comes France
an immobile
and pertinent thus
returns through water
harp and flute and heat
bends horizon from
they don't answer
a pervasive clear
I took this picture
ample bay glass
or pinched vantage
the sign warms
through slippage very
soprano ice column
he writes at desk
the Denver Tosca
up here out there
was patient even
birds on deck
I quit
large columnar columns
as if water could
ice tray
four impresses nine
called bleeding winces
he so
and makes small talk

a cogent article
plus four plus extra
leaf damage but
the illusion of shattering
arresting heat
thanks I'll not
and behold novelty
progress keeps lever
this last.

# IV

SOKRATES: Hail Ion, enviable rhapsode wherefrom are you come?

ION: From Epidaurus where I won another contest.

SOKRATES: You know I envy you reciters always well dressed and hanging out with poets, especially Homer whose lines are nice but whose thought's sublime.

ION: True enough, not to know Homer is not to know.

SOKRATES: Will you embellish him in our purview awhile?

ION: Indeed crowns trumpets laurels annointments fall on my head you've come to the right place.

SOKRATES: Now I'm just a dumb hick, hardly worth talking to, but answer me one thing don't all poets say the same thing? Why Homer and not, say, Hesiod?

ION: I can't figure it out. When others mention others I frankly doze but Homer wakes me esplain this riddle.

SOKRATES: No problem. First it's not from knowing that comes your knowledge of Homer but from a power divine. What you say is not what you say but what is said through you, agreed?

ION: You've got the floor.

SOKRATES: A poet is a light and winged thing, never composed until he's drunk a draught and then he soars. It's not by art he sings of arms and men but by that chain he shares wlth one he'd heard somewhere before. And like a chain you too are linked to Homer just as some are linked to Orpheus and others to Musaeus, and when the light foot hears you you either dance or doze.

ION: And so we reciters read the readers, if I read you right.

SOKRATES: Right, I figured you'd come round. But wait. Let's say you're saying some Homer one Tuesday, and you come to the part where Odysseus unmasks himself before the suitors, you know the part?

ION: I'm all mouth.

SOKRATES: Or where Achilles rushes Hektor aren't you transported, aren't you an action?

ION: I'm hardly in the room. My hair stands up, my heart's in another planet.

SOKRATES: So there's your audience, eyes brimming; they ache because you ache. Man thinks he lives by art alone but muses tend to trickle-down their inspiration you but breathe through. And your audience is the final link in that great chain the muses sing through as if to say "we hope you like our song but liking's not our concern but yours." In short you're not the speaker but the spoke.

ION: Well put, but you can't tell me that though I'm mad when reading Homer I can't praise in him the things I know.

SOKRATES: On which point?

ION: On every point without exception.

SOKRATES: Even on those points upon which you have no knowledge?

ION: And what matters might those be?

SOKRATES: Chariots, for example. What are those lines where Nestor speaks to Antilochus, his son, warning him about the turning post in the race in honor of Patroclus. I'll recite them, if you like.

ION: No, give me the reins where I own the car:

> At the post lean left
> of the rest
> then goad the off horse
> with hand
> give him free rein
> and at the turn
> let near horse come close
> enough to graze the stone
> but don't hit it.

SOKRATES: Very good. Now on the matter of chariots whom do you trust, Homer or Horser?

ION: Horser no doubt.

SOKRATES: Because who better to know the art of horse than he who rides? Homer's but a lexicon of horsey things, but only those who ride know how to hold the reins. In other words each art speaks whereof it knows, do you not agree?

ION: I admit of differences among things which separately I know not.

SOKRATES: Precisely, for in many poems we take for granted what we're given, yet admitting differences we can't adjudicate at all. So if the rhapsode knows not the art of spinner, charioteer or general yet speaks of spinning, riding and leading troops how can he claim to speak in their behalf. Or better put, what does a rhapsode know?

ION: Well, a rhapsode knows the kind of speech a general makes or a woman the kind of wash she describes we're talking power over diction here.

SOKRATES: And having power over diction is having power over women and animals?

ION: Unquestionably, I say with trepidation, Sokrates.

SOKRATES: So whoever is a rhapsode is also an able general.

ION: They're both a single.

SOKRATES: And thus a general is also a rhapsode by such logic?

ION: Nope, it doesn't work the other way around.

SOKRATES: Why not? You are the most able rhapsode in Greece—and the ablest general as well?

ION: You said it, not me. What can I say, I learned it all from Homer.

SOKRATES: So we Athenians should hire you, knowing all you know not only of Homer but of general things.

ION: I'd take the job.

SOKRATES: But (and here's the catch) if you know by art what you couldn't possibly know by craft are you not like Proteus simply art twisted round a likelihood? And if you, as you say, speak winged words without the benefit of reason how can you in honesty speak these praising words of Homer. Choose, therefore, how you will be called by us a man unjust or a man divine?

ION: Simple: to be divine is just.

SOKRATES: And a lovelier title it is, Ion, to be divine in simple mindedness than be artful in praising Homer.

# V

In other dialogues I've argued that poets corrupt the morality of the
State, but here, for the sake of argument, I claim that the only good
poet is one who knows what he's talking about. Ion may be a good
reciter of Homer, but he doesn't know from poetry—precisely
because there's nothing there to know. Poetry is a cipher of every-
thing everyone has said already and to repeat it is only to validate
this very fact. To analogize, however, is to have your Ion and your
dialogue too. As I said somewhere in the Gorgias, speaking of
rhetoric, these arts have no subject but themselves; they feed on
other arts but have at their center only words. To propose that
poetry involves knowledge is rank folly and is why poets should
leave theory to those with academic positions or at least a federal
grant. With these credentials one can dissolve categories, split hairs
and contradict oneself at will. Although it has gotten a bad name in
recent years, Science offers the critic the very authority he needs to
assert these truths and to do so without having to get his hands
muddy at the public trough of so-called popular opinion. He can
rise above the contentions of ordinary dialectics by pointing to the
flaws in vulgar speech, all the while claiming solidarity with those
unfortunates who use it. Ion loses the argument every time by his
inability to apply such authority to an art which more properly
belongs to translators: since they can't produce anything of their
own, they merely reproduce what others give them. Ion thinks that
to know how to read is to know what one reads when in fact he is
un-read by his own assertions. I believe in a separation of church
and state, so to speak: the man who believes and the man who
thinks are one centaur, and no association of sensibility will be of
much use except to the makers of mirrors. It is worth upholding the
distinction between art and life because in so doing you get to buy
shares in both. Which is precisely why, although I've been known
to stand behind the arras and listen to Ion do his rendition of
Penelope at the well, I must publicly renounce the watery words he
uses. Language is all superstructure; it can't do anything of its own,
which is why I have made such a profession of professing nothing.

At least in this way, when the Revolution comes, I won't be stuck with hemlock as my only recourse. Who knows, I might be made Secretary of Defense for my aptitude at manipulating a press conference.

## VI

Then fog minus hills
four as before or
woman marked man
speech without word and
one speaks
hardly closed
because from Greece
a protean wind
but irrelevant nor
advances skirting shores
piano and drum and
refracting vicinity by
because they don't hear
a partial static
while you stood there
limited inlet mirror
either expansive focus
the sign cools
by tension hardly
baritone mist arras
she fingers knife
the Dallas Norma
out there up here
will approach odd
absence of birds in
you begin
miniscule redundant globes
but ice might
fire pan
five is impartial to
sent coagulate I smile
she that
but elaborates

the independent article
minus nine minus less
leaf damage and
the fact that coherence
releases wind
recrimination he'd better
but ignores repetition
repetition loses to button
that first.

# VII

It means the same this writing so why write?

Yet he attempts to dissolve a complex web by referring to the trees from which it hangs.

A tree is a complex web ln whose branches live creatures who emerge in the crepuscular hours to look upon us with dark eyes.

They met not to consolidate a position but to consume a possible hamburger.

In between the first and second descriptions a tense had changed even though both refer to the same event.

He refuses to admit the object as in any way determining the shape of sound a flute makes reaches his ear and continues to the other side.

The speechwriter was fired for having implied that the candidate was not the origin of his speech.

The dialogue would never have occurred if the heat had not forced the two friends out into the country where they heard the chirping of the cicadas.

Having spoken only to the other's answering machine for several days he was surprised to encounter the actual voice of his friend and promptly hung up.

They imagine that stories have their origin in action but we who have heard no such stories must simply interpret the language of birds.

They showed us the photograph of the miniature city modelled on the actual city in which they had stayed which included a perfect replica of the miniature city within the miniature city and so forth.

And Thoth came to him and exhibited his various arts which included drafts and dice as well as writing and said that this discipline my King wlll make the Egyptians wiser and will improve their memories.

He is unclear whether the first time he saw his father was in he living room or in the photograph of the living room in which his father appeared in uniform.

Only a spoken word can have a father, hence he is one of the logoi, one who argues.

Once the four great stones with the Greek word for "wave" roughly etched in each were put in place the students followed suit by carving their own names into the surface.

Once it was new and then it became time.

# VIII

Back then, recently, not so long ago, once upon a time he wrote.

In other words no theory can be produced without considering the making of me, myself and I.

He heard persons walking past his closed car as leaves rustling in the wind.

"I made her so mad she was burning" caused her to underline "she was burning" she was so mad.

He achieved a metaphysics that only materialism could contain.

An earlier judge had been easily confirmed, but he unlike the current candidate, had had the good sense not to write his opinions in a material form.

A tree-like grid imposed itself on the actual tree, allowing him to understand an architecture the leaves obscure.

A tree like God impressed itself unnatural tree she saw the towers the leaves obscure she read and in them cast adrift alternate measures the dance.

Her greatest pleasure before discovering Paris had been diagramming sentences oddly enough.

Our age came in because of a vast displacement.

Achieving mastery implied having read the book prior to discussing it, though many gained theirs by assuming others hadn't and opening their mouths.

In the interim between one section and the next the caterpillars had turned into moths and now flitted brightly among skeletal branches.

In paradise solitude is painful to a social mind.

The letters contained references to persons now scattered about the landscape who are at this point and by displacement largely textual and from henceforth wlll be known as A, B, C, et cetera.

I miss the typewriter the cautious approach to the right margin tail on the letter q western vistas in the logo of Remington bell.

Memory was invented somewhere back in the eighteenth century but you wouldn't know it.

Many of the missing details could be obtained by phoning the individuals in question who invariably contradicted what others had said earlier history is a perpetual phonecall.

He was a partisan of many Gallic systems.

The famous critic was on his way to deliver a speech on desire when he met a Dante scholar on a bridge words were exchanged they came to blows he arrived to his lecture late with a black eye.

Light had taken on new meaning now that conifers and oaks had replaced sage and mustard though eucalyptus are ubiquitous in both places causing neighbors much uneasiness.

He wrote out of a desire to stand in the midst of history like a tall tree with the great spirit blowing through him on its way to the present.

Do you mind if I share your table?

Poetry lifts the veil from the hidden beauty of the world and makes familiar objects be as if they were not familiar.

Death is a condition, not a promise.

This book is printed by McNaughton & Gunn in an edition of 1000 copies, twenty-six of which are lettered and signed by Michael Davidson.